Everything, You

Written by R.R. Vincench

Illustrated by Maria Holubeck

NONESPOT
PUBLISHING
(an imprint of Nonespot, LLC)

First edition 2022
Text copyright © 2021 Robert R. Vincench
Illustrations copyright © 2021 Nonespot, LLC

All rights reserved.
This book, or parts thereof, may not be reproduced in any form without permission in writing from the publisher. The scanning, uploading and distribution of this book via the internet or via any other means without permission from the publisher is illegal and punishable by law.
Please support the author's and publisher's rights. Thank you!

Any resemblance or likeness to any person or event in this story is purely coincidence.

Our books are printed on demand wherever our printer deems it necessary. Usually, this is in the country where the book is ordered. Most or all orders in the U.S.A. will be printed in the U.S.A.

Please visit us online at nonespot.com, where you can expand the book experience, discover our full library, and more.

Hardcover Edition ISBN 978-0-9960264-6-8
Softcover Edition ISBN 978-0-9960264-5-1
ebook ISBN: 978-0-9960264-7-5

Dedicated to my beautiful Ania
You are everything.
Love,
Daddy

CONNECT WITH US

Empty. Resting. Unseen light.
Vast potential. Starless night.

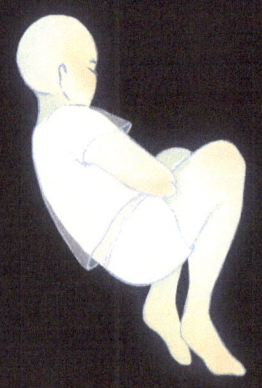

Suddenly—a dot appears.

The start of all things. Far and near.

A flash explodes. Birth of light.

Stardust. Rocks. Endless worlds.
Suns and stars. Whirls and swirls.

Some with air, water, life.

Places like Earth, where we call home.
A place among many, but a world alone?

This is how we have come to be.
With time comes all the things you see.

Rivers run.

Oceans gleam.

All of nature can be seen.

Flowers, forests, mountains, rain.
No two sights are quite the same.

Life evolves. Critters, beasts.
Some with tails... wings... teeth...

Bugs and animals of all kinds.
Some get smarter along with time.

Dolphins and humans. Things between.
Intelligent entities not yet seen.

Humans are free from their first day.
Connected, yet living in our own way.

Such thoughtful and creative things.

We dream and wonder. Laugh and sing.

We strive to improve. We learn and teach.

There's hate and kindness.

War and peace.

We break and build. We fear and love.

We seek below and reach above.

We find amazing places to be.

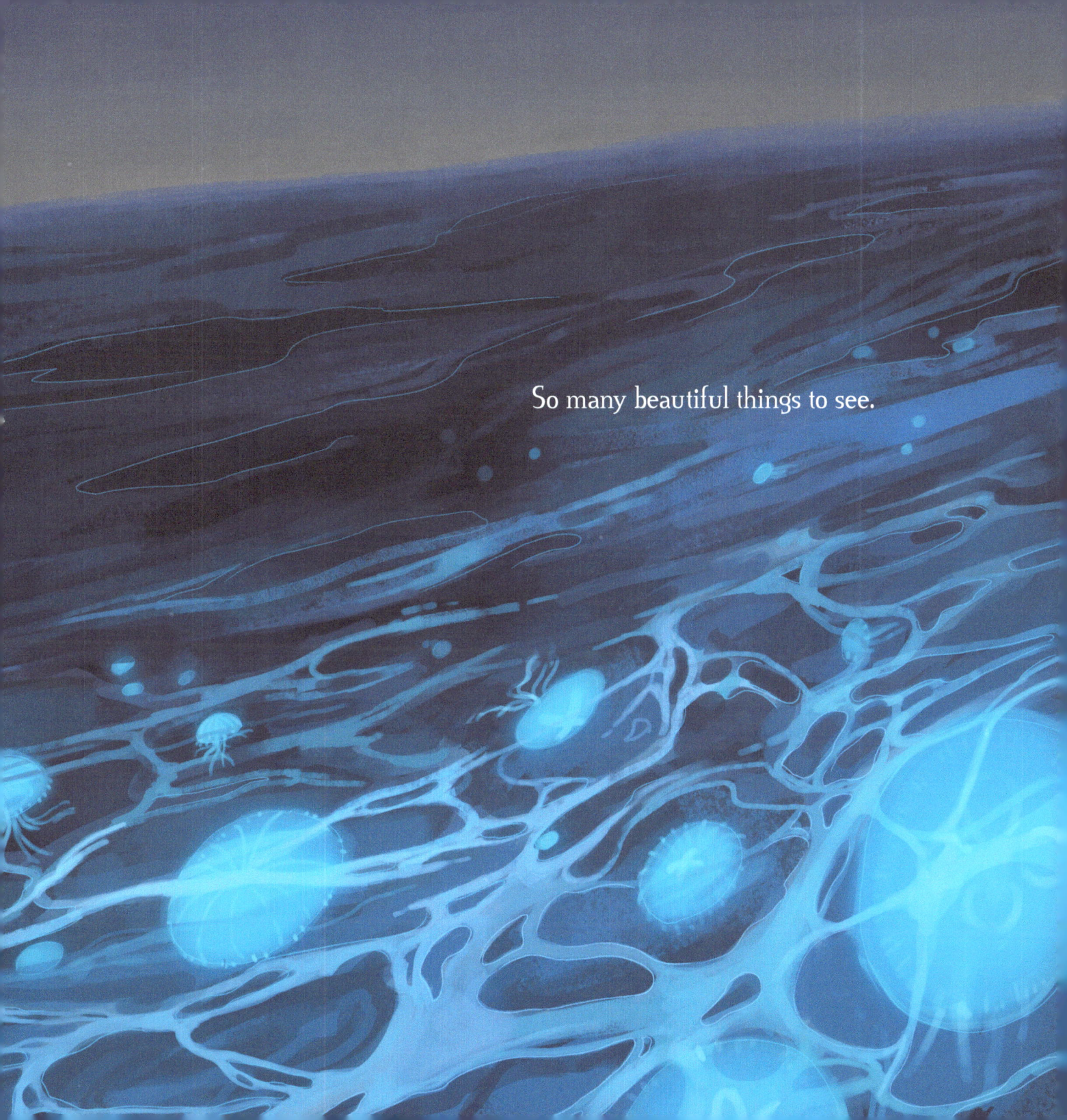

Here, beautiful reader, is where you are.

Connected to all who've ever lived.

A passionate heart. A special mind.
Made of stuff from the birth of time.

and always be true.

Thoughts for Little Thinkers

Don't end the experience with just the story.
Here are some learning opportunities and ideas
to explore the book even further.

1. Which page is your favorite?
   What is it about that page that you connect with most?

2. Throughout this story, there are all kinds of creatures.
   Go through the pages, find the many creatures, and identify
   what they are. For extra fun, what sounds might they make?

3. You can find opportunities to count almost everywhere.
   Find the following things throughout the book, and count
   how many there are on the page: JELLYFISH, ANTS,
   BUILDINGS, HANDPRINTS, FALLEN BOOKS, DOLPHINS,
   LETTUCE, GARDENERS, SHARKS, and more.

4. Find the page with sharks and seagulls that informs us
   of critters and beasts having "tails... wings... teeth."
   What other critters and beasts can you think of that have
   these physical traits?

5. The page with ants, a crow and an elephant shows us
   that some bugs and animals "get smarter along with time."
   What do you think the crow is doing with the stick?
   What are some smart things you've seen an animal do?

6. The page with people gardening together tells us:
   "We do great things, with room to grow."
   What do you think they are growing? Do you grow food?
   What else can people grow? Your confidence? Your mind?

7. What does this story inspire you to think about?

CONNECT WITH US

For more on this book
and our other offerings,
please visit us online at:
www.nonespot.com

SCAN ME

www.ingramcontent.com/pod-product-compliance
Lightning Source LLC
Chambersburg PA
CBHW060809090426
42736CB00003B/214